D1295087

FISH FINNED AND GILLED ANIMALS

BY SUZANNE SLADE   ILLUSTRATED BY KRISTIN KEST

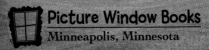
Picture Window Books
Minneapolis, Minnesota

Thanks to our advisers for their expertise, research, and advice:

Jim Stoeckel, Ph.D., Assistant Professor
Department of Fisheries and Allied Aquacultures
Auburn University, Auburn, Alabama

Terry Flaherty, Ph.D., Professor of English
Minnesota State University, Mankato

Editor: Shelly Lyons
Designer: Lori Bye
Page Production: Melissa Kes
Art Director: Nathan Gassman
Editorial Director: Nick Healy
Creative Director: Joe Ewest
The illustrations in this book were created with oil paints.

Picture Window Books
151 Good Counsel Drive
P.O. Box 669
Mankato, MN 56002-0669
877-845-8392
www.picturewindowbooks.com

Photo Credits: page 22, (top row, left to right, and repeated uses),
iStockphoto/George Peters; U.S. Fish & Wildlife Service; Shutterstock/
Picsfive; iStockphoto/Vebjørn Karlsen; iStockphoto/Helle Markussen;
Shutterstock/Paul-André Belle-Isle; iStockphoto/Eric Isselée;
Shutterstock/Steffen Foerster Photography; Shutterstock/Gregg
Williams; iStockphoto/Le Do.

Printed in the United States of America.

 All books published by Picture Window Books
are manufactured with paper containing at least
10 percent post-consumer waste.

Library of Congress Cataloging-in-Publication Data
Slade, Suzanne.
Fish : finned and gilled animals / by Suzanne Slade ; illustrated by Kristin Kest.
p. cm. — (Amazing science. Animal classification)
Includes index.
ISBN 978-1-4048-5523-6 (library binding)
1. Fishes—Classification—Juvenile literature. 2. Fishes—Juvenile literature.
I. Kest, Kristin, ill. II. Title.
QL618.S57 2010
597—dc22   2009003291

TABLE OF CONTENTS

A World Full of Animals 4

Breathing and Hatching 6

Bones and Blood 8

Scales and Fins 10

Wet, Watery Homes 12

Classes of Fish 14

Hungry Fish 16

Strange Fish 18

Fish in Our World 20

Scientific Classification Chart 22

Extreme Fish 23

Glossary 23

To Learn More 24

Index 24

A World Full of Animals

Millions of animals live on our planet. Scientists classify animals, or group them together, by looking at how the animals are alike or different.

Six of the more familiar main groups of animals living on Earth are: mammals, birds, reptiles, amphibians, fish, and insects. Let's take a closer look at fish.

All fish have certain things in common: they have gills, they are vertebrates, and they live in water. Most are also cold-blooded, have scales and fins, and hatch from eggs.

Breathing and Hatching

So how do people know which animals belong to the fish group? All fish have special parts called gills. Gills allow fish to breathe underwater. Water passes over the gills. Then the gills take in oxygen. Some fish also use their gills to take in food called plankton.

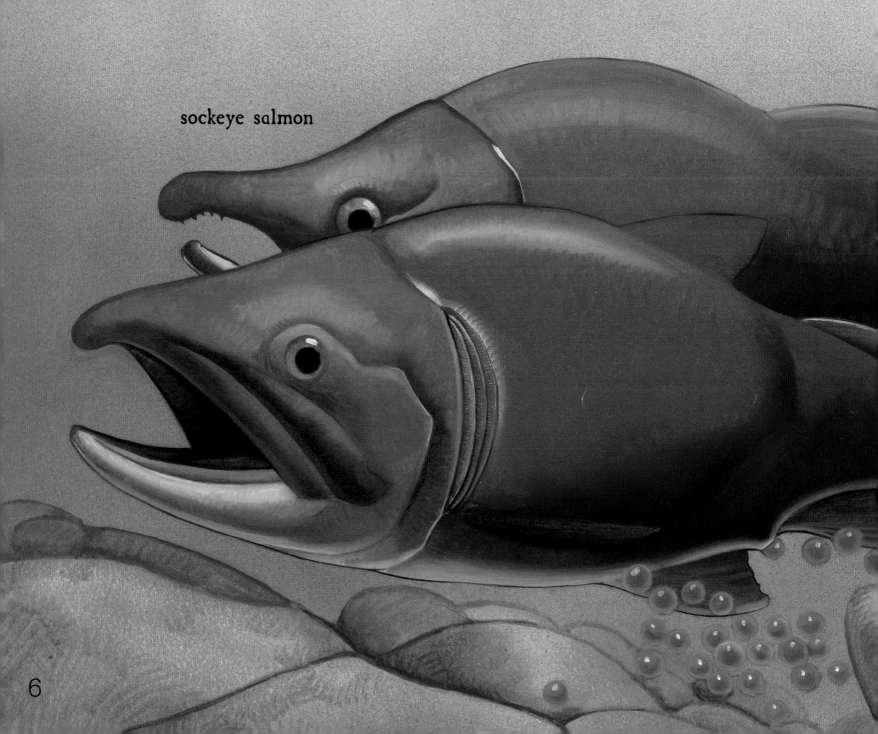

sockeye salmon

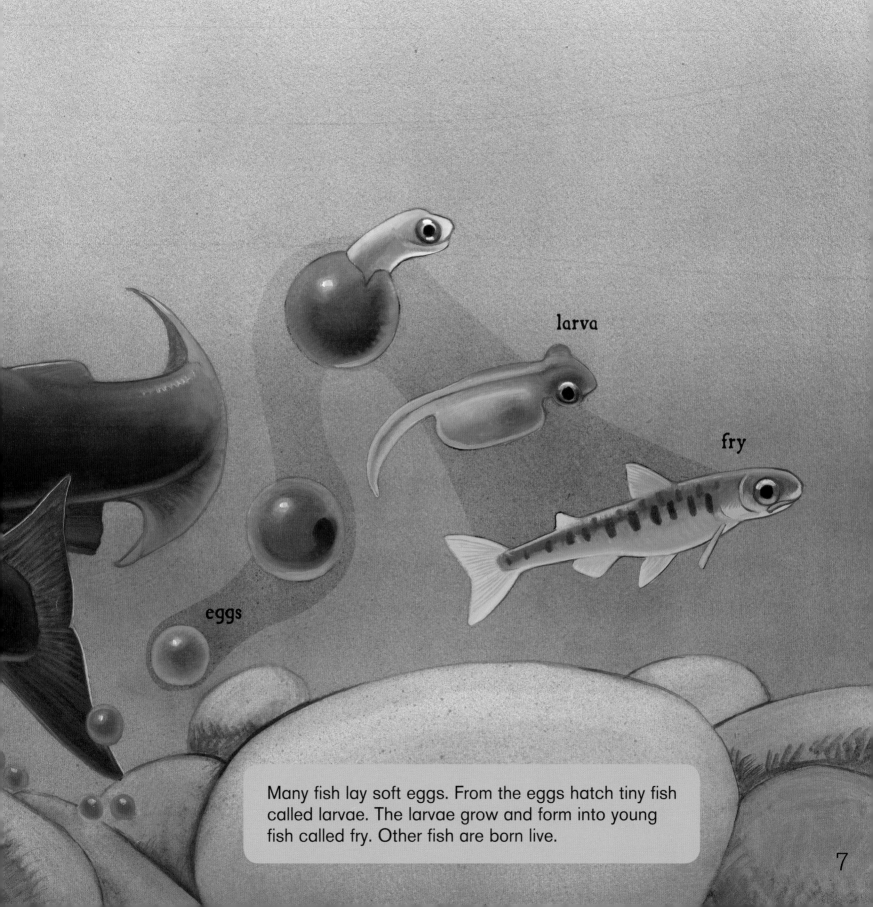

larva

fry

eggs

Many fish lay soft eggs. From the eggs hatch tiny fish called larvae. The larvae grow and form into young fish called fry. Other fish are born live.

7

Bones and Blood

Fish have some other features that are not easy to see. They are vertebrates. That means they have a backbone. Most fish are also cold-blooded. That means their body temperature changes with the temperature of the surrounding water.

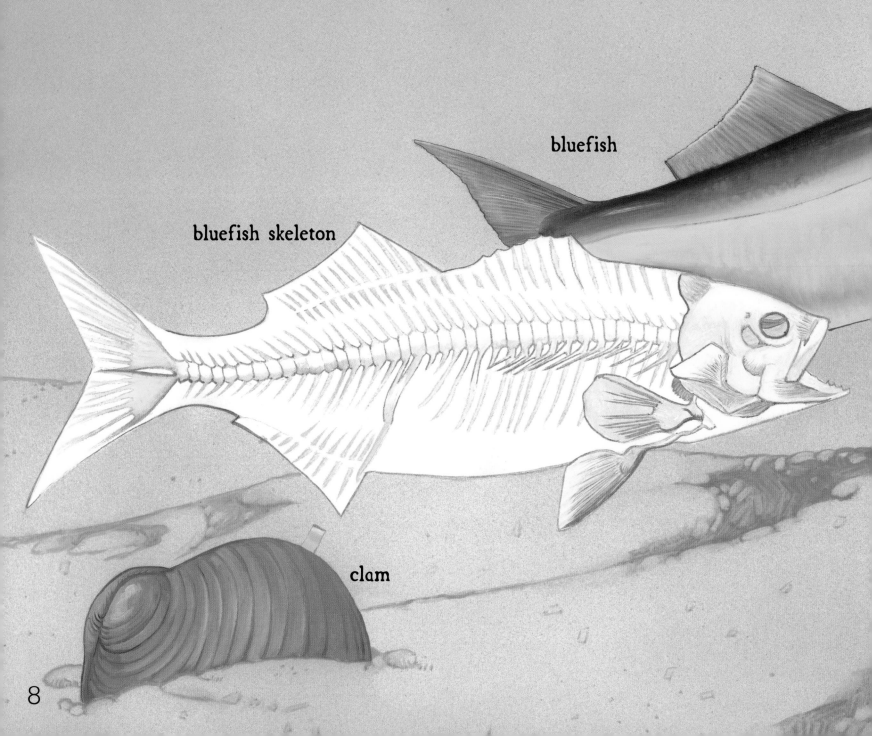

bluefish

bluefish skeleton

clam

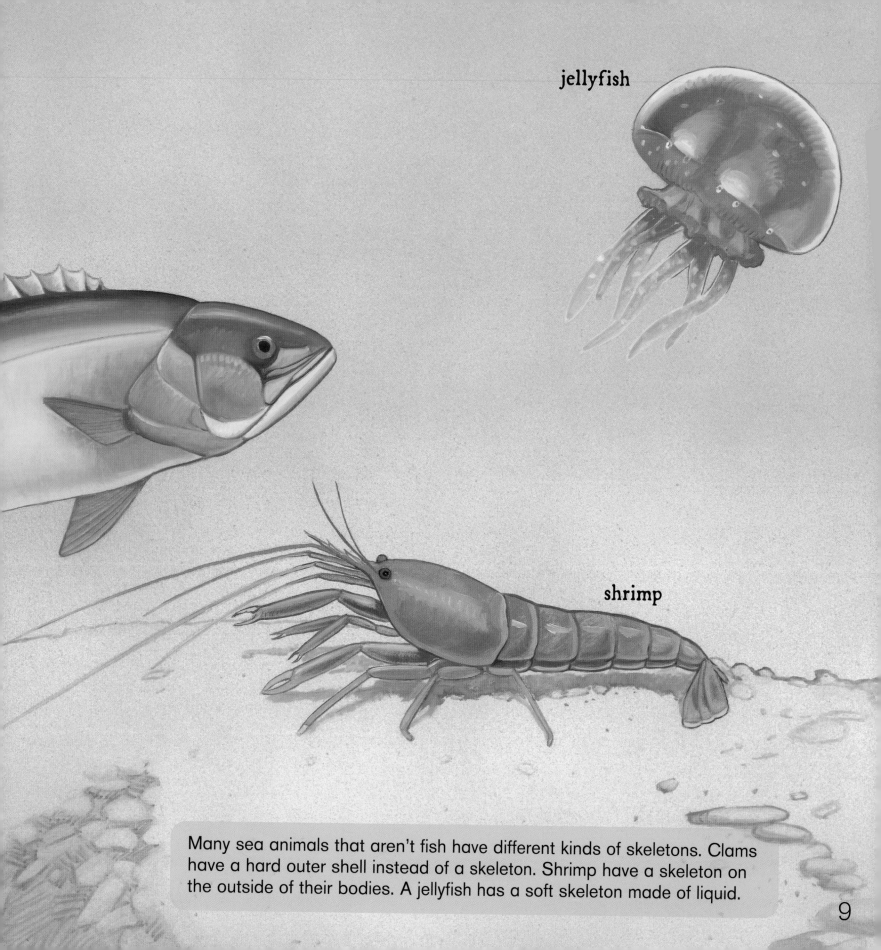

jellyfish

shrimp

Many sea animals that aren't fish have different kinds of skeletons. Clams have a hard outer shell instead of a skeleton. Shrimp have a skeleton on the outside of their bodies. A jellyfish has a soft skeleton made of liquid.

Scales and Fins

Most fish have hard scales on their skin for protection. Most fish also have seven fins to push, stop, and steer themselves through the water. Two side fins, called pectorals, are used for steering. The caudal fin on the end of a fish's tail gives the animal power and speed. The other four fins on the top and bottom of the body help keep a fish upright.

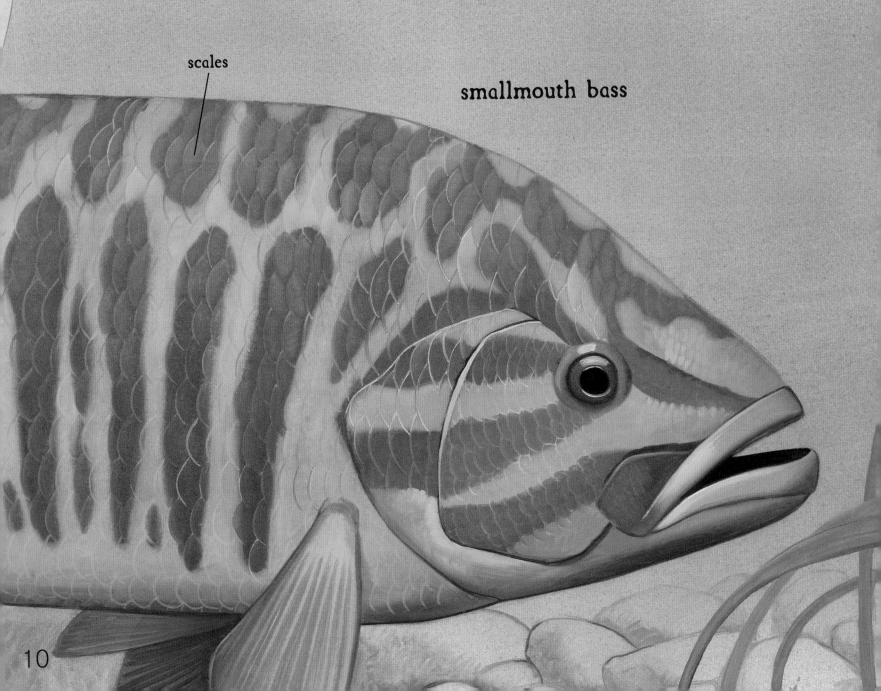

scales

smallmouth bass

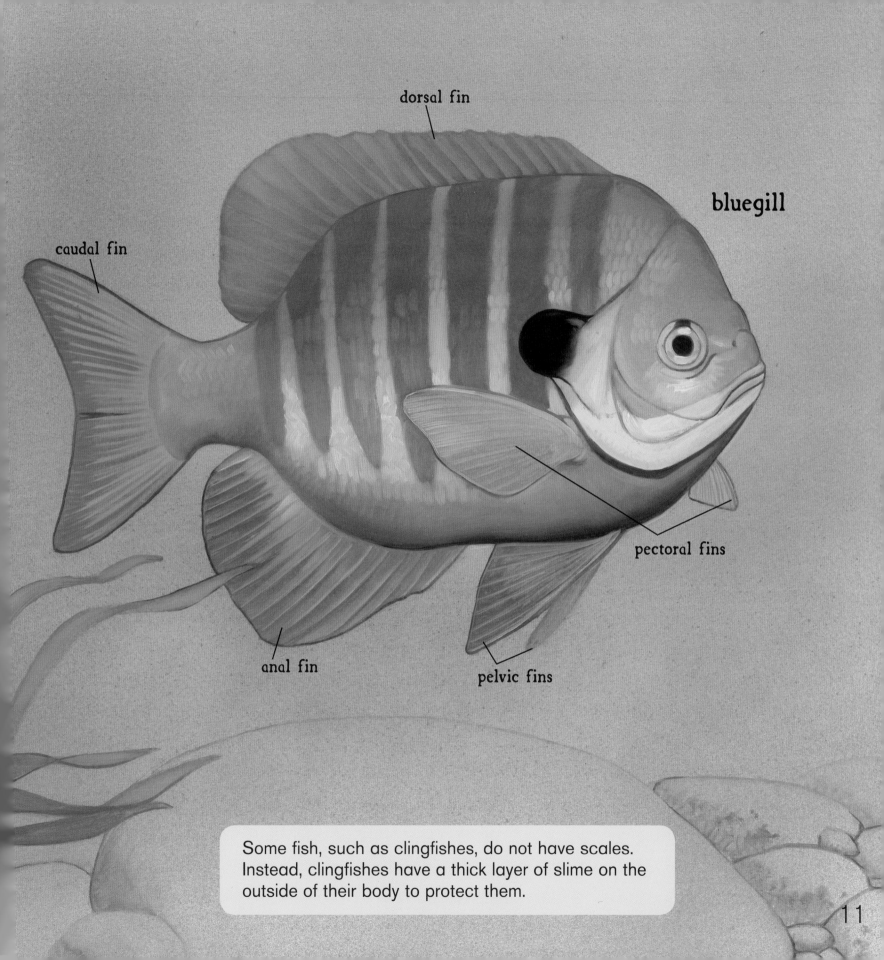

dorsal fin

bluegill

caudal fin

pectoral fins

anal fin

pelvic fins

Some fish, such as clingfishes, do not have scales.
Instead, clingfishes have a thick layer of slime on the
outside of their body to protect them.

11

Wet, Watery Homes

Fish live almost anywhere there is water. Many kinds of fish, such as sharks, butterflyfish, and cod, make their homes in salty seas.

white shark

copperband butterflyfish

Bass, trout, and other fish live in freshwater lakes, ponds, and rivers. A few fish, such as Atlantic salmon, live in both saltwater and freshwater.

largemouth bass

There are more than 27,000 different kinds of fish in the world. They make their homes in warm coral reefs, icy mountain streams, leafy underwater forests, and many other places.

13

Classes of Fish

Fish are divided into three smaller groups called classes. The largest class is bony fish. Bony fish have skeletons made of hard bones. Another class is called cartilaginous fish. These fish have skeletons made of cartilage. Cartilage can bend, but it also keeps its shape.

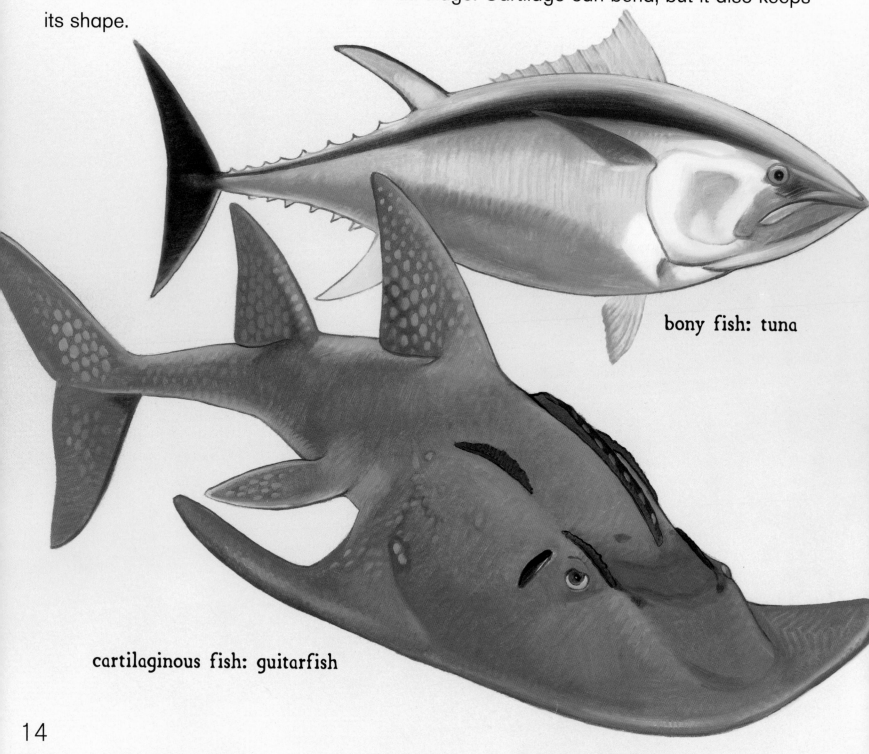

bony fish: tuna

cartilaginous fish: guitarfish

The third class is called jawless fish. These fish also have cartilage skeletons. But they do not have jaws for chewing. Instead, they use their round mouths to suck up food.

jawless fish: lamprey

More than 90 percent of fish are bony fish. Tuna, catfish, and goldfish are bony fish. Cartilaginous fish include guitarfish, sharks, and rays. Jawless fish are long animals that look like snakes. Lampreys and hagfish are examples of jawless fish.

Hungry Fish

Most fish eat other animals. But some eat plants, seeds, and even mud. Many fish, such as piranhas, sharks, and groupers have sharp teeth to catch and chew their prey.

piranhas

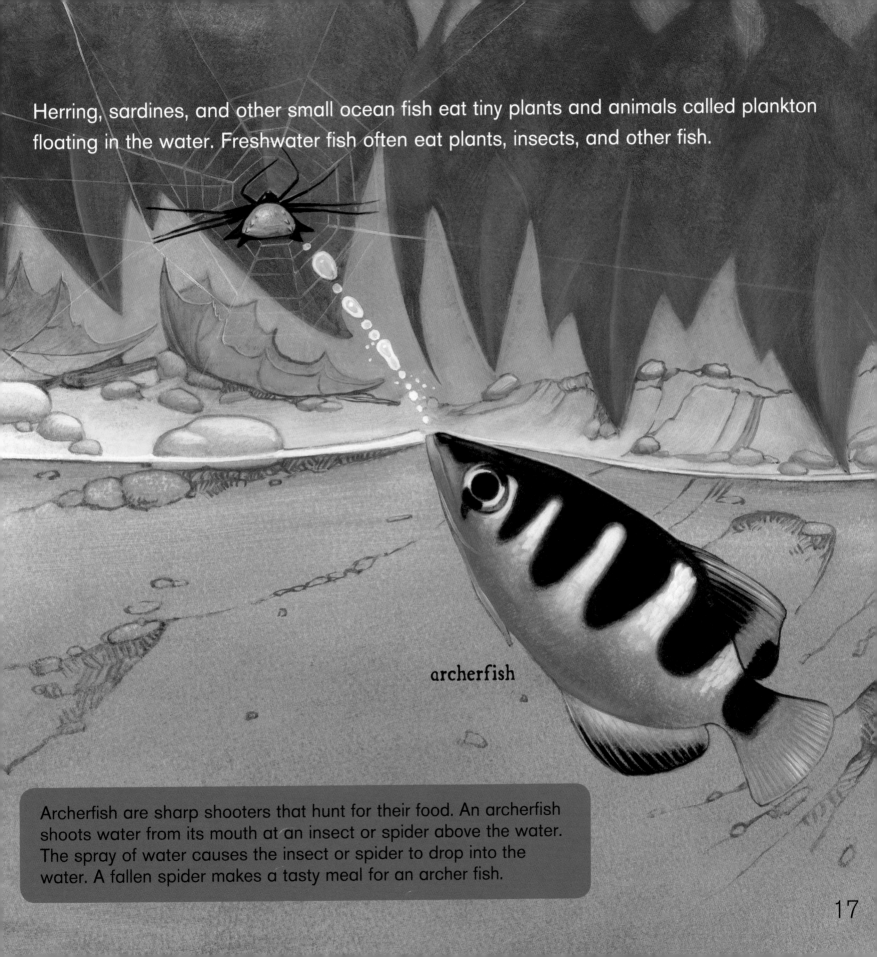

Herring, sardines, and other small ocean fish eat tiny plants and animals called plankton floating in the water. Freshwater fish often eat plants, insects, and other fish.

archerfish

Archerfish are sharp shooters that hunt for their food. An archerfish shoots water from its mouth at an insect or spider above the water. The spray of water causes the insect or spider to drop into the water. A fallen spider makes a tasty meal for an archer fish.

Strange Fish

Some unusual sea animals belong to the fish family. Surprisingly, sea horses are fish. These slow swimmers have gills, fins, and a bony skeleton. Hagfish are long, snake-like fish. Their skin creates slime to help them escape from enemies.

sea horse

Flying fish have fins that work like wings. These fish can leap out of the water and soar up to 4 feet (1.2 meters) in the air.

flying fish

Some sea animals look like fish, but are not. For example, dolphins and whales are not fish. Instead of breathing through gills, dolphins and whales breathe air through a blowhole on their head.

Fish in Our World

Fish have lived on Earth for more than 450 million years. They come in many shapes and sizes. People often keep beautiful fish as pets in small aquariums in their homes. You can look for different kinds of fish in ponds, oceans, or aquariums near you. It's fun to learn more about amazing animals called fish!

hammerhead shark

bluefish

clownfish

hagfish

sea horse

blennies

guitarfish

butterflyfish

clownfish

21

Scientific Classification Chart

The animal classification system used today was created by Carolus Linnaeus. The system works by sorting animals based on how they are alike or different.

All living things are first put into a kingdom. There are five main kingdoms. Then they are also assigned to groups within six other main headings. The headings are: phylum, class, order, family, genus, and species.

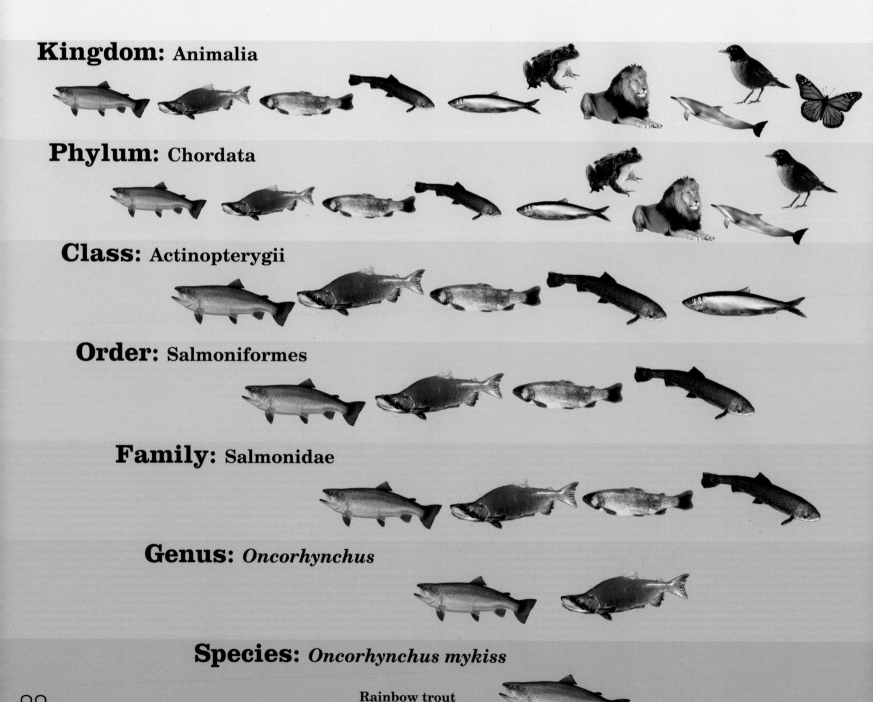

Kingdom: Animalia

Phylum: Chordata

Class: Actinopterygii

Order: Salmoniformes

Family: Salmonidae

Genus: *Oncorhynchus*

Species: *Oncorhynchus mykiss*

Rainbow trout

Extreme Fish

Largest fish: The largest fish in the world is the whale shark. This enormous fish can grow up to 40 feet (12.2 m) long and spends most of its time in deep ocean seas.

Smallest fish: The tiniest swimmers are a type of carp called Paedocypris fish. They live in swamps in Sumatra. An adult Paedocypris fish is about less than half an inch (1.3 centimeters) long.

Hottest fish: The desert pupfish is one hot fish. It can live in water that is more than 100 degrees Fahrenheit (37.7 degrees Celsius)!

Fastest fish: Most people believe the fastest fish in the world is the sailfish. This speedy swimmer has been clocked at 68 miles (108.8 kilometers) per hour!

Longest name: The fish with the longest name is found in waters near Hawaii. Although this small fish's common name is reef triggerfish, it also goes by the Hawaiian name of Humuhumu nukunuku apua'a. Try saying that three times fast!

Glossary

anal fin—a fin found on the underside of a fish; it helps keep a fish upright

cartilage—the strong, bendable material that forms some body parts on humans and animals

caudal fin—a fin found on the tail of a fish; it gives a fish power and speed

cold-blooded—having a body temperature that changes with the surroundings

dorsal fin—a fin found on the back of a fish

gills—parts of a fish that help it breathe underwater

oxygen—a gas that people and animals must breathe to stay alive

pectoral fins—a pair of fins found just behind a fish's head; they help control the direction in which the fish is headed

pelvic fins—a pair of fins found on the underside of a fish; they help keep a fish upright

plankton—very small plants and animals that drift in lakes and oceans

prey—an animal that is hunted and eaten for food

scales—small pieces of tough skin that cover the bodies of some animals including reptiles and most fish

skeleton—the bones that support an animal's body

vertebrate—an animal that has a backbone

To Learn More

More Books to Read

Lundblad, Kristina, and Bobbie Kalman. *Animals Called Fish*. New York: Crabtree Pub. Co., 2005.

O'Hare, Ted. *Fish*. Vero Beach, Fla.: Rourke Pub., 2006.

Pyers, Greg. *Why Am I a Fish?* Chicago: Raintree, 2006.

Internet Sites

FactHound offers a safe, fun way to find Internet sites related to this book. All of the sites on FactHound have been researched by our staff.

Here's all you do:

Visit *www.facthound.com*

FactHound will fetch the best sites for you!

Index

bones, 8, 9, 14, 18
classes, 14, 15, 22
cold-blooded, 5, 8
eggs, 5, 7

fins, 5, 10, 11, 18, 19
food, 6, 15, 16, 17
fry, 7
gills, 5, 6, 18

homes, 12, 13, 20, 23
larvae, 7
scales, 5, 10, 11

Look for all of the books in the Amazing Science: Animal Classification series:

Amphibians: Water-to-Land Animals

Birds: Winged and Feathered Animals

Fish: Finned and Gilled Animals

Insects: Six-Legged Animals

Mammals: Hairy, Milk-Making Animals

Reptiles: Scaly-Skinned Animals